Loving Moments

Poems Celebrating Love's Journey

DEBORAH ANN MARTIN

Loving Moments: Poems Celebrating Love's Journey

By **Deborah Ann Martin**

ISBN:
eBook: 978-1-966771-21-0
Soft: 978-1-966771-23-4
Hard: 978-1-966771-24-1

www. Survivinglifelessons.com

Second Edition

This book is dedicated to those who helped, inspired, and encouraged me.

Table of Contents

Attraction

"Granted, physical attraction is what gets you in the door. But there has to be something beyond that to want to keep you there."

-Author: Jaci Burton

Eyes for You

Don't know what to do

I only have eyes for you

Going where you'll be

Hoping you'll see me

Should I talk to you

Don't know what to do

Will you talk to me

If I keep going where you'll be

On the Hunt

As I walk,

I smell the sweet

scent of you. My eyes look

around hoping to catch sight. I try

to be casual about it. As I walk forward the smell

 gets weaker. So, I turn around hoping to catch sight. It's like

I am in a trance hopelessly following. How can a

scent be such a powerful aphrodisiac?

How can your scent drive me

crazy enough to follow

it just to catch

sight?

smile

hoping to catch your eye

i smile as you go by

eyes lock as you go by

you smile as you catch my eye

Potential Date

A potential date

Visually stimulating

With words that appeal.

Awaited Kiss

A longing, desire tingles within

As I caress your skin

Nervous anticipation for a long-awaited kiss

Eyes close as the face slowly leans forward

Will our lips meet with heavenly perfection

Or will you turn with complete rejection?

Flirt

Think not; let love flow

Know you don't need to try

Why not laugh

Or give a wink

First Kiss

As they walk to the door,
She wonders where he stands.
She had an enjoyable date.
She feels attracted to this man
.

He's never felt this way before.
Being together is what he was aspiring for.
He doesn't know if he should wait.
Waiting is causing perspiring

Both wonder what the other is waiting for.
Both anticipate the other's plans.
With an ever-increasing heart rate,
He begins to think of a plan.

He eases toward her more.
He feels his sweaty hands.
He softly talks and gets closer to his date.
He eases in as far as he can.

He doesn't know what is in store.
But he gives in to his yearning demands.
No longer can he wait.
Their first kiss is better than they had planned.

Budding Romance

A Glance

A Smile

A Word

A Beginning

You're on My A-List

adventurous, affectionate, amazing

authentic, awesome, adorable

adored, attentive, astounding

attractive, accomplished, amiable

admired, assembler, astonishing

agreeable, angler, admirable

appreciative, adoring, amazing

artistic, aroused, amicable

Catch Your Heart

The twinkle in his eyes

The laughter in his smile

The confident walk

The quick-witted comments

The charm

Thinking About You

I

Smile

When I

Think about you!

♡

Male Friend

When things were rough,

You showed me I was tough.

You always seemed to care.

Your friendship you shared.

When you sang your lovely songs,

It gave a sense of belonging.

My feelings seemed to matter.

You helped when life grew sadder.

When I was happy or blue,

You were there to see me through.

Sometimes you would hug like a bear.

I felt as though someone cared.

Can't let feelings grow stronger

For fear of not being friends any longer

It is better to have you near

Then take the chance that I fear

Just Friends?

We're just friends.
  But you are so kind and compassionate.
We're just friends.
  I love how I feel when I am with you.
We're just friends.
  I wonder if you like me.
We're just friends.
  I can see myself being with you.
We're just friends.
  You look so good; I love the smile.
We're just friends.
  We have so much in common.
We're just friends.
  You make me laugh.
We're just friends.
  We're there when we need each other.
We're just friends.
  If I wanted to be with you, I might get hurt.
We're just friends.
  Are you kinda interested in me?
We're just friends.
  If I like you and you don't like me that way?
We're just friends.
  We kissed.
You said, "we're just friends."
  I'm confused.
We're just friends?

Gift of Me

I may not be who you want me to be.

I may not be anyone but me.

I may not be a musician.

I may not be a physician.

I may not be a sports star.

I may not play the guitar.

I may not be worth millions.

I may not be a famous civilian.

I may not be one with incredible talents.

I may not be the type who's gallant.

I am able to give the gift of me.

I am able to help someone in need.

I am able to share a smile.

I am able to make someone feel worthwhile.

I am able to stop and listen.

I am able to pay attention.

I am able to help with a meal.

I am able to express how they feel.

I am able to do more than you see.

I am able to give the gift of me.

A Smile on My Face

You put a smile on my face

Knowing you love me

Meeting at our special place

You put a smile on my face

Our lives interlaced

As happy as can be

You put a smile on my face

Knowing you want me

Interested

I never knew
You were interested in me too!
What do we do?

Snorkeling

Beautiful blue sky and fluffy white clouds
Clear blue water that shimmers
Like diamonds
Mark a beautiful summer day on the
Puerto Rican Shoreline.
Declan enters the refreshing blue water
Adorned with his snorkeling gear.
His tan body and fine physique
Show off his swimming shorts.
As he looks back on the shoreline
His grin makes the girls watching swoon.
Their eyes remain fixed as they
Watch his perfect form
Rock with each wave
Each longing to be the water.
Declan loves the outdoors.
He cares only about
Going with the flow of the ocean
And seeing a natural beauty below.
 He avoids the sharks, barracuda, and fire coral.
Schools of tropical fish swim by the colorful
Coral below. Lobsters peak their heads
Out from the Rocks.

As he dives to pick up a starfish,

The girls gasp in delight.

One small Multi-colored tropical fish swims

Around his body,

The starfish's legs cup his hands.

While he swims around, he notices

The green seagrass moves like

There is a gentle breeze.

For Declan, nothing matches

The beauty of the world below.

As he surfaces, his dazzling smile and

the setting sun hold the girls in a trance.

As he returns to the shore

Walking through the crashing waves.

For the girls, nothing matches

The beauty of the world above.

Unique

You're so unique to me

You helped set the real me free

I'm not expected to be perfect

I'm not expected to change

I respect you and your opinions

And you respect me and my opinions

You're as Special as Can Be

You're as special as can be
Because you let me be me
You're willing to try the foods I like
You're eager to try the activities I do
In turn, I am anxious to try new things with you
It's nice that you have fun with me

You're as special as can be
Because you let me be me
We don't always see eye to eye
You don't try to control my thoughts
You talk them out with me
But you don't get mad if I don't see as you

You're as special as can be
Because you let me be me
I don't have to pretend to be someone
I don't have to think like someone
It's nice having someone who gets me
The real me

You're as special as can be
Because you let me be me

First Date

Starting to date brings so much anxiety and fear.
The stress can even bring a tear.
There's so much anxiety when going on a first date.
You are excited and can't wait.
As time draws near,
The internal questions add more fear.
What do you wear?
How do you style your hair?

If he gives me a creepy vibe, be crazy, or makes me annoyed,
Will my emergency call work and be deployed?
Will I be able to make sure we are never alone?
Will I spill something on myself or trip since I am accident-prone?
If I like him, will we go on another date?
If I don't, how do I tell him his fate?
What do I do if awkward silence happens on the date?
Should I be early, or should I be a little late?

Wow, I have so many questions to ask.
While I am performing my predate task.
I am so nervous maybe I shouldn't go
I have some time, I know.
As I drive to the place,
Panic sets in, and my heart starts to race.
How can I work thru this?...ah-hah. Call a friend!
I call the one I know I can depend.

We laugh as I begin to share.
She talked me through it all the way there.
I get there a little early and begin to wait.
He must be running late.
What if he doesn't show?
How long do I wait? I do not know.
I need to kill time while I am able.
What is acceptable while you wait at the table?

There he is at the door.
He matches his picture and more.
When he comes over, do I sit or stand?
He introduces himself and holds out his hand.
I smile and introduce myself too.
Now, what do I do?
I start talking about the venue.
Then I ask him what he likes off the menu.

We begin to talk and share.
Before long, I don't seem to have a care.
Stress and anxiety go away.
I am relaxed for the rest of my stay.
What do I think about this man?
Do I want to see him again?
What does he think about me?
I guess I will have to wait and see.

Snuggling

Snuggling together

Watching the crackling fireplace

With a glass of wine

Wendy's Bouts-Rimés

Skip realized he was late for his first **date.**
How could he be a **ditz** when Sally is a blitz?
In a **splash**, he made a quick dash.
To the florist knowing the **power** of a flower
Adding chocolate would be **twice** as nice.
Sally left her **house** in her favorite white blouse.
Sally went down the **ally,**
In her **car,** to a local bar and grille.
She cringed when the car hit a **toad** in the road.
She got out of her car and noticed **oil** on the soil.
She shrugged; no need to t**oil;** it was only a little oil.
She sat in the bar to **wait** and wondered why Skip was late.
She said, "You're Late, **Mate.**"
He said jokingly, "Take a **chill** pill."
"Pretty **dove**; these are for you, my love."
Out came chocolates and **flowers,** and he saw its powers.
Her heart did **melt** when he expressed the love he felt.
After dinner, they took a **walk** and had a nice talk.
They walked about a **mile** through the garden tiles.
The **light** was no longer bright.
They knew it was the **night's** end, kissed, and said goodnight.

Why Do You Make Me Love You?

It's been so long
The walls built strong
Windows and doors barred
Protected by a guard

Brown-eyed, brown-haired knight
Laughed at the wall in delight
That wall is no match for me
Just wait and see

Stories of adventures untold
Two bricks fell
Two bricks were replaced
Wall stands strong

Songs of old
Three bricks fell
Three bricks were replaced
Wall stands strong

Laughter in the air did ring
Four bricks fell
Four bricks were replaced with extra mortar
Wall stands strong

The fun he did bring
Seven bricks fell
Three bricks were replaced
Wall is unsteady, but sound

A gentle touch from the hand
Seven bricks fell
Three bricks were replaced
Guard pushes back and stands firm

A kind and gentle soul
Windows crack
Doors crack
Again, the guard pushes back

Comfortable and feeling whole
One side comes crumbling down
Twelve bricks were replaced
Guard stands sound

Thoughts of so many qualities are the same
Bricks put back up fall again
Windows and doors open wide
Guard works harder and continues to try

Gentle kiss
Half the wall topples down
One brick laid at a time
Guard works harder and won't admit defeat

Persistence and declarations of love no longer dismissed
Walls continue to crumble down
Windows and doors crumble down
Guard leaves in utter defeat

Progression

Gentleness

Tenderness

Holding me tight

Feeling right

Smell of scent

Hearts descent

Endearment

Enchantment

Femininity

Masculinity

Want and Desire

Hearts on Fire

Love and ecstasy

Continuing legacy

Passion

"If passion drives you, let reason hold the reins."

-Benjamin Franklin

Caress

Sitting on a blanket

    Under the shady apple tree,

The lovers hold

    Each other.

He gently caresses

    The side of her face.

Then holds it as he

    Leans forward to

Caress her lips

    With his tender kisses.

As he stares into

    Her eyes, he softly

Caresses her arms.

    Then whispers caressing

Words into her ears.

Heat

A soft caress warms the heart.

One kiss ignites the soul.

Passion explodes, and fire runs through the body.

Giving In

A gentle kiss turns to fire.

The eyes are longing with desire.

Hands move in a soft caress.

It sets the heart beating in duress.

Excitement rages within.

Until finally, they both give in.

You Drive Me Senseless

As I stare into your eyes, I draw my face closer. The sound of your alluring voice is like a Siren's call. The smell of your cologne takes my senses to a heightened level. Touching the side of your face is like touching a burning ember. Your awaiting lips taste like sweet honey's nectar. The feel of your lips ignites a fire deep within me that I have been longing to feel. My hands begin to wander, wanting to touch you. The possession inside of me wants to keep touching you. To continue touching and never stopping. Never letting go. As your hands slowly move down the length of my body, my passion grows hotter. I melt into your embrace as your hands continue to take me in. My legs grow weak under your constant touch. The fire raging within me burns out all thoughts. The only thing that remains is longing and desire.

Begins With a Thought

Continual thoughts

Intimacy

Longing to be in your arms

Desire running through my veins

Lustful moment

Give into your charms

Lose control

Fall into your arms

Passion that cannot be denied

Passion was never so strong

Leaves continual thoughts

Passion

Pining that changes perspective

Ardent affection

Strong and barely controllable emotion

Sexual desire

Intense deep interest

Overwhelming feelings

Notion that becomes an obsession

Hidden in the Dark

Only enjoying each other hidden in the dark
A man who is kind and descent
A woman hopelessly devoted
Words of passion and desire

Spending time together hidden in the dark
Time together is delightful.
Food eaten together is delicious.
Words of passion and desire

Secret kisses are done hidden in the dark.
Neither can decide,
A love hidden but not demoralized.
Words of passion and desire

Love is made hidden in the dark.
Hidden but exciting and delectable
Or open and allowed to deepen
Words of passion and desire

Decisions are made hidden in the dark.
Open and deliberate
Passion, hunger, love, devotion
Words of passion and desire

Love's Fire

Love's fire

Passion, desire

Kisses that send heat to

My loins. Yearning like no other.

Ache, want

Romance Is in The Air

Romance is in the air

Life doesn't have a care

Heavenly bliss

In the kiss

Being held with tender care

Joy and happiness everywhere

Smiling and laughter

Compliments that flatter

Loving so much

Caress in a touch

Looking into each other's eyes

The whole world passes by

Nothing like a budding romance

To make the heart leap and dance

Portal to Soul

Look into my eyes
My heart and soul are revealed
Passion and desires

Doting Heart

In the gentle touch of your hand

A loving kiss

A caring hug

In the sensual embrace

A warm smile

A romantic jester

In the admiration of your eyes

A soft caress

A flirty wink

In the affectionate words

A devoted life

A teasing laugh

In the tender holding of hands

A yielding cuddle

A doting heart

Embrace

Your love's firm embrace,

Your deep passionate kisses

Flames burning desires.

Storm

It's a beautiful day
For a stroll along the bay.
I walked along the shore,
Thinking I wanted more.

       I'm afraid I might go over the ledge
       If I come too close to the water's edge.
       The soft breeze caresses my face,
       Causing my heart to race.

The rippling water looks so refreshing.
Fear and excitement are enmeshing.
The water whispers a plea
To come closer and see.

       When the sand gets hotter,
       I feel the pleasure of the water.
       Wet, squishy sand is sweet
       When the water swirls around my feet.

I want to feel more
So into the water, I want to explore.
Giving into all the charms
Embraced in its arms.

       Floating to the rhythm of the sea,
       The gentle cadence feels like ecstasy.
       The waves gently retract,
       Then roll softly back.

Clouds start to form
A single-cell storm.
Wind-blown hair
Goes everywhere.

    The sea waves retract,
    And thunderous waves come crashing back.
    Excited as each wave overtakes me,
    Breathless as I emerge from the sea

I can hear the water hitting the shore,
Begging for more and more.
As time seemed to suspend,
The storm quickly ended.

    The clouds parted
    To reveal a beautiful sunset started.
    I walked back to the shore.
    Then, I watched the sea once more.

Carpe Diem

Subtle glance
Accidently touching hands
Conveniently being near
Laughter in the ear
Take the chance
Start the dance
Lose them if you're a bother
Or lose them to another
Better to risk all with a try
Then later, ask why
Take the chance
Ask them for romance
Seize the Day
Take the opportunity to laugh and play
Don't let fear get in your way
Today has the potential for a great day
Take the chance
Start the dance
Don't wait
Ask before it's too late
You never know
Love might have an opportunity to grow
Take the chance
Ask them for romance

Fuel

I have tried to ignore

The fire that burns deep inside

It's all-consuming

My thoughts, my words, my actions

You're the fuel that feeds the fire

Love Letters

Each stroke of the pen

Expressions of passion and love within

Distance and time keep you away

Longing to be together each day.

Words cannot truly express the longing.

Each stroke of the pen

Gives words of love until

We see each other again.

Thoughts of you fill my day

Waiting until we can

Hold each other in a sweet embrace.

You Scare Me

You scare me because I never thought I would love being with anyone again. I enjoy our time together, laughing and talking while doing activities. *You scare me because I never thought I would trust again.* I have felt so comfortable telling you my problems and secrets that you have become my best friend. *You scare me because you are the first and the last thing I think about at night.* You're the first person I think of calling when something good or bad happens. *You scare me because loving you this deeply and passionately puts my heart at risk.* While in your sweet embrace, I never want our time to end. *You scare me because I never wanted to feel this vulnerable.* Loving you, wanting you, desiring you, needing you means that I would be devastated losing you. *You scare me because you are one of the most caring, loving, and wonderful people I know.* Because of who you are, the love, desire, and passion make me want you even more. *You scare me because I love how I feel with you.* When I am with you, I feel loved, cared for, special and beautiful. *You scare me because I didn't want to get hurt again.* You scare me because when I am with you... I am willing to take a risk.

Day-To-Day

Passion in your day-to-day life

Gives you energy and vitality

To extend to your partner.

Renewed

Passion gone

Nothing to act on

Tired, problems and duress

Filled my mind with stress

Busyness of life

Caused me strife

I took a mental break

That I deserved to take

In my head

We were in bed

Picture the love in my heart

It was the first place to start

My imagination started to run

Then the excitement had begun

I wanted to tell you how this went

So, a text was sent

Thoughts were now on the way

Passion was renewed today.

Overdressed

I lose myself in those eyes

That look at me with hunger

Leaving me feeling overdressed

Beginning or End

You weren't the kind of person I would date when I first met you. I gained some new information every time we spoke. I observed a warm and caring man with the fortitude to overcome his flaws despite them. Despite not looking, I discovered something I had no idea I could find. We find things that we both enjoy doing. We are different. We accept the differences because we fit just like a left hand holds a right hand. Interlaced, they are strong. Our differences give strength when one is weak. We can embrace our differences. We are two parts of a whole that fit perfectly together. We fit together like two perfectly matched pieces of a puzzle. The attraction grows stronger with each passing day. The more about you I learn, the more I want to be with you. There are days when wanting you is all that's on my mind. It's a thirst that can't seem to be quenched. My mind wanders to the kiss. The sweet taste of a kiss burns fire through your veins. It's a kiss that clears my mind, allowing me to concentrate solely on being in your arms and never leaving them. I want to feel your strength in your gentlest touches. Your touches leave a trail of heat and passion that leave me wanting more. Wanting more and knowing we have to wait until I know in my head that it is worth the risk of being hurt or sinking deeper into emotional dependence. Someday, when I am willing to take the risk, I'll be ready to lose myself in pleasure. At least in those moments, I will feel the excitement, energy, and passion that come from knowing and wanting someone for so long. I will lose myself in the pleasures only you can provide in those moments. Then, we will see whether it's the beginning or the end. All I know is that right now, all I can think about and desire is being in your arms.

Three Times the Passion

*P*ining, *P*artiality, *P*ersuasion

*A*ffection, *A*llegiance, *A*dulation

*S*atyriasis, *S*alaciousness, *S*exual

*S*ensitive, *S*ense, *S*entiment

*I*mpression, *I*ntense, *I*nfatuation

*O*bsession, *O*utlook, *O*pinion

*N*otion, *N*ecessity, *N*oticed

Raging Tornado

Passion without thought

is a raging tornado

that can destroy lives.

When I Met You

Your eyes are a pretty brown

And a personality that was round.

Your body was a golden tan.

Your luscious lips should have been ban.

God gave you a nice set of cheeks

To go on that perfect physique.

You romanced me by the lake under a tree.

It was there that you stole my heart from me.

You filled it with joyous times

And took away the bitter sighs.

Loneliness never came my way

For your gentle hands caressed it away.

Around you, I never felt the urge to cry.

Problems may have arisen, but on you I could rely.

During the day, you are filled with compassion.

At night, it turned to passion.

At first, the fire in your eyes was dim.

But I could feel the warmth within.

There was something in the touch of your gentle hand.

It would set my heart to your command.

You carefully pulled me near.

Then gently whispered in my ear.

As my blood pressure got higher,

The fire in my body got hotter.

A soft kiss got bold.

The love exchanged became untold.

Longing and Desire

As you pull me closer, I feel the heat rising

within. My senses go

wild as I breathe in your sweet smell.

Your touch leaves a trail of heat on my skin. My brain

loses focus as you whisper words of passion into my ears.

Longing and desire are all I can feel.

I want to feel my body as close to yours as possible.

I lose myself in the sweet taste of your kisses.

Longing and desire are all I can feel.

I no longer have conscious thoughts.

I cannot get enough of you.

All I want is more! I can't get enough

Longing and desire are all I can feel.

Love

"*The only thing we never get enough of is love; and the only thing we never give enough of is love.*"

-Henry Miller

Immeasurable

I have a love so deep

and intense that it surpasses

all time and distance. Circumstances

will either put up a wall of protection so

it will not be hurt or damaged, or events will

help the love to grow. Being in a friendship

or intimate relationship, these feelings

will always be there. The difference

is whether they can be

acted on or not.

Hearts Desire

Love is splendor; love is kind.

Hold onto true love, for it is hard to find.

Some may bring passion and fire.

Only one can bring my heart's desire.

There can only be one who is this dear.

Cherish them and keep them near.

Nurturing

Love takes nurturing

    as an emerging flower

        needs water and sun.

Loving Effects

It's beautiful to find your one true love.

It feels like a miracle from above.

There is a connection you have never felt.

It makes your heart melt.

Your thoughts drift as never before.

You always wait for a call or a knock at the door.

There is an excitement you can't seem to shake.

At night, you constantly think as you lie awake.

You enjoy giggling and playing.

You enjoy having someone listen to what you say.

This companion is there to enjoy special times.

When together, you hear the ringing of chimes.

A feeling like this is the best experience of your life.

So do not bury it under daily strife.

Love Me

I love you.

I love the me I

Am with you.

At This Moment in Time

At this moment in time,
Lying in your arms
The world seems miles away.
Everything seems so right.
Emotions are complex to describe
It makes me feel so alive.

At this moment in time,
I've never loved you
As much as I now love you.

At this moment in time,
I've never loved another
As much as I love you.
The past has gone away.
Walls came crumbling down.
Our time seems to stand still.

At this moment in time,
Precious memories are made
As pure love flows our way.
Feelings that are so strong
Like I've never had.
Part of me wants to run.

At this moment in time,
I'll embrace our special time
As pure love flows our way.

Gift of Love

On the pillow is his smell.

He's been here, I can tell.

In the bathroom, his hair lies on the sink.

Inside, I feel our special link.

I sit in his shirt, reading his book.

I know that this man has me hooked.

I cannot focus since he came.

I think of different ways to write his name.

I feel a sense of awe in the air.

I constantly think of us as a lasting pair.

I know that this is made in love.

This man is a gift from God above.

Loving Feelings

Each kiss feels like heavenly bliss.

Your love feels like it comes from above.

I know you care, and I trust you'll be there.

The loving gleam in your eye is in my dreams.

It is hard to beat the feeling of being complete.

My soul feels like it is on a happy roll.

There is an inner peace that will not cease.

I enjoy taking walks to talk.

We are willing to show that love as it grows.

This loving feeling in my heart, I pray it doesn't depart.

Love

Spirits uplifted

Hearts beating rapidly

Shared Love

Rejoicing together

Souls joined

Happy Home

Complete

~Love~

Complete

Home happy

Joined Souls

Together rejoicing

Love Shared

Rapidly beating hearts

Uplifted Spirits.

Show

I know that I may not always show it.

I know that I may not always say it.

But you should always believe it.

I Love You!

Love is Blind

Loving you is like newly fallen snow,

Everything is covered and looks beautiful.

United Hearts

My mind drifts to our time together.

Time away seems like forever.

Our love keeps a unique bond when apart.

Invisible strings tie our hearts.

We long to be in each other's arms,

To be under the spell of love's charms.

There's magic in our time together

That keeps us bound forever.

You'll always be a part of me.

It just seems like destiny.

We share a love that grows even when apart.

We're friends and lovers with united hearts.

Cannot Separate

A love so strong

Desire so great

Time and distance

Cannot separate

There's Nothing I'd Rather Do

When I'm in the midst of a busy day
And I want a smile to come my way
There's nothing I'd rather do
Then just think about you.

When my life is full of stress
And it seems to be a mess
There's nothing I'd rather do
Then just hold you

When time passes by
And when I don't know the answer why
There's nothing I'd rather do
Then to talk with you

When there's joy in my life
And there's no apparent strife
Then there's nothing I'd rather do
Then to smile with you

When I want someone to go somewhere
And like some enjoyable company while there
Then there's nothing I'd rather do
Then to share them with you

When I want happiness in my heart
And know I never want to be apart
Then there's nothing I'd rather do
Then to fall hopelessly in love with you

Touched My Heart

The love we share has touched my heart.
As I lie in your loving arms,
The whole world around me stands still.
There is magic in these moments.

When my body is drawn closer,
The love we share touches my heart.
Your fingers glide across my skin
Leaving a warm heat in its wake.

Snuggling closer against your chest
My heart races hearing yours' beat.
The love we share has touched my heart
Binding us with the special bond we share.

Each moment in your caring arms,
Makes me feel happiness and love.
Nothing compares to the comfort in your arms.
The love we share has touched my heart.

To Love and Be Loved

To Love and Be loved
Is the theme of songs, poems, and stories
Battles have been fought
Wars have been won and lost
All for the sake of love
All for the search for a true love

To Love and Be loved
This driving need causes isolation
Bad experiences cause fear
Some try to live without it
But deep inside is emptiness and longing.

To Love and Be loved
Is a need for human touch and intimacy.
Without it, we all wither away first inside
But eventually, it will cause us to die.

To Love and Be loved
There's nothing more fulfilling than finding the right person
There is no greater hell than to live with the wrong person

To Love and Be loved
It is at the core of every human's existence.

Intimacy of a Relationship

The hugs and kisses
The sly grins
Quick-witted jokes
While I do the dishes
Kissing me as you leave for work

    Hanging out watching you work
    Lying in each other's arms, talking
    Smile at each other
    I want the intimacy of
    A relationship with you

My head on your lap
While you play with my hair
Hugging me from behind me
Random hugs
Just staring into my eyes

    Buying one flower when you're out
    Just to let me know you're thinking of me
    Caressing
    I want the intimacy of
    A relationship with you

Doing an activity I want
Even though you hate it
Simply touching me as you walk by
Sharing dreams and planning them out
Doing activities together

Occasional back massage
Playing with my hair
Warming up my car on a winter's day
I want the intimacy of
A relationship with you

Occasionally as you walk in from work
Search me out and kiss me
The compliments
Gently hold the side of my face
The apologies

Holding hands
Sitting on a porch swing together
Just hanging out together
I want the intimacy of
A relationship with you

Pure and True

Love pure and true

Time for holding you

Whispers of sharing

Enjoyment of caring

Making memories that last long

Sweet melodies of a song

Laughter in the air

Romance delicately shared

The loving heart of two

The pleasure of love pure and true

Sweet Love

Love's sweet

Fragrance fills the

Air affecting all those

Around. Bringing us happiness.

Sweet Love

Together

Walking along the seashore

holding hands, leaving two sets

of footprints in the warm sand.

Love is in the air.

Lost in Love

Lost in love

Happiness never known

Lost in love

A remarkable, exuberant feeling

Shared emotions that have grown

Pleasant memories that are sown

Lost in love

Love

L
O
V
E

is patient

is kind

does not envy

does not boast

is not proud

does not dishonor others

is not self-seeking

is not easily angered

keeps no record of wrongs

does not delight in evil

rejoices with the truth

always protects

always trusts

always hopes

always perseveres

never fails

Keeper

Keeper

    Trust, Honesty, Respect, Independent, Loyalty, Laugh

Keeper

Keeper

    Companionship, Communication, Compromise,
Commitment, Compassion, Considerate

Keeper

Part of My Heart

It's   hard
Finding the right   one for me. It was
Hard for me to believe.   It was hard for me to
Conceive. To finally   find an honest man. Who
Loves me for who I am. We   laugh, and we share. We are
Two sides of a heart. One is left, and the other is the right. But
the things in the middle that we share we can hold on tight.
Our similarities hold us together. Our differences make us who
we are and what we love about each other. The skills we lack
the other holds. Making us a perfect whole to help face
problems proud and bold. We are perfectly well-rounded
people instead of being two unique circles that are all about
self. We open ourselves up like the top of A heart. Some
times coming together is simple and easy as the top.
Other times, our differences make it harder and it
takes longer to come together. It's a longer path
like the bottom. It's about give and take. Like
when the heart is folded, each has its part.
Two equals that make a whole. Equal
but different. It takes both parts
to make a heart. Without it,
the heart is broken.
Thanks for being
Part of My
heart

Love Not Perfection

Love knows I am not perfect.

Love knows I need someone who loves me

Despite me

Because of what they see in me

Love doesn't try to make me an ideal image the world sees

Love doesn't try to mold me into a mini them

Love knows the bad in me

Love sees only the good in me

Love isn't about perfection

Love is about loving despite imperfection.

New World

I wandered aimlessly through life.

I thought I had everything I needed.

I thought I had everything I wanted.

You showed me a side I never knew existed.

I felt feelings I never knew I could feel.

You opened my heart to a brand-new world.

Now that I know this incredible world,

I don't ever want to lose it.

I didn't have everything I wanted.

I didn't have everything I needed.

I am no longer wandering aimlessly through life.

I want the kind of life that you showed me.

I want to always feel that kind of love with you.

Forever

"Grow old with me, the best is yet to be."

– Robert Browning

Proposal

Looking back in time, it amazes me how well you knew me. It was such a surprise that I didn't see it. You said you wanted to plan a weekend trip. I was so excited, not knowing when or where. I asked if there was anything I should plan to do with my hair. What should I wear? With a grin and a laugh at my inner little girl's happiness, you say casual, comfortable clothes. Where we were going, who knows? I set out for the task. I did as you asked. When the time arrived within the hour, you showed up at my door with a flower. It was such a sweet thing to do. It was exciting to go on an unknown adventure. It was great not to plan but to have someone plan for me. We drove for a couple of hours. What was so amazing about those hours was that you made a music playlist of songs to listen to. Not just any songs... This playlist included songs that had meaning. As each song played, you told me why you chose that song. I cried as I listened to each song. They were songs about us, how beautiful you thought I was, my personality, our fun times, and songs you thought referred to our future together. I cried because I was so happy and had never felt so loved or wanted ever in my life. We pulled up to a nice hotel. I thought... well, you know what I thought. We check in and go to our room. In our room, we had a room with a view. It was a spectacular view. When we got in there, there were 11 more roses to go with the one you had given me when we left. You told me you had stuff for me to take a nice relaxing bubble bath. You got the tub ready and lit the candles placed in the room. You put some soothing music on. Then kissed me softly and said, you'll be waiting for me, and to take my time. When I came out, you had a candlelit dinner sitting on the balcony. You lit the candle in the center of the table. You moved the relaxing music from the bathroom to the balcony. You removed the tray with our food. I love seafood. You had two seafood dinners delivered to our room. It was a fantastic meal. After we ate our dinner, you asked me to slow dance with you. You held me close. The knock at the door startled me. I jumped... and well... and I cussed a little in surprise... not anger. You laughed. It was another food delivery—our dessert. We sat down at the table. After the hotel staff left, you poured us some wine. Then you opened the metal dome. You had my favorite dessert, cheesecake. In the center of my piece was a beautiful ring... just slightly into the cake. You told me such beautiful words about a future and a life together. You professed your love and devotion. I could picture that life with you. I believed that you loved me and would be good for me and with me. I could imagine life and kids with you. A friend, a lover, and someone to share the good and bad times with... When you asked, I said yes! Definitely yes! You took the ring out, licked the cheesecake off, and placed the ring on my fingers. Then the kiss... wow... what a kiss. I will fill that kiss on my lips for a long, long time. Thinking about it still makes me smile. It was a memorable and magical night. When the weekend was over, we dreaded returning to work. However, we now look forward to the future and hope to know each other for a lifetime. We were excited to tell everyone we knew the good news. You gave me an intimate proposal and a public celebration. I love you and look forward to a lifetime together, creating memorable moments for each other. I love you now and forever.

In Your Arms

Waking for the first time in your arms
I felt safe from being hurt, safe from harm
I have this overwhelming happiness
I love just lying here watching you breathe
I know that for the rest of my life
That I get to do this
Excitement and the newness of our commitment
Kept me restless all night
But it was alright
I was able to feel your lingering touches
I could lie in the dark and remember
The hours before
I was able to feel your strong arms around
Me as you snuggled close
As I softly play with your hair and face
Just watching you makes my heart race
Wow, you're mine forever
This is not just a casual fling or
A relationship for years that isn't going anywhere
I get to love and be loved
We get to start our new lives together
As you slowly begin to wake
I can't wait for the love we are about to make.

Building a Relationship

Building a relationship requires both people to tear down old walls and let individual expectations go. Then follow the master's blueprints for laying down a firm foundation for a solidly built home.

God should be the foundation, and love the cornerstone. The rest should be built together, one brick at a time. When a brick is laid, fix it before you build further. Otherwise, it will remain that way either permanently or until you tear down the walls to that point. Then you start building up again.

Soul Mate

A touch
Being Near
Contagious passion
Deep Love
Ever-changing
Forever together
Good feelings
Hearts Afire
In Love
Joyful beloved
Keep vows
Loving-kindness
My strength
Never-ending friendship
One Love
Promises kept
Quivering knees
Respect Mutually
Smile Often
True Love
Undying love
Venerate sweetheart
Wild for
Xtra romantic
Yearning heart
Zealous supporter

Marriage

Friend

Companion

Lover

Soul mate

Supporter

Advisor

Teacher

Solid

A solidly built home

Will stand the test

Of time.

Colors to Life

When home feels dull and drab,
add color to the walls
and add some green plants.
When a relationship feels dull and drab,
add some fun activities
and add some laughter.

My Love

My love,

When I met you, I thought I knew all about love. Finally, I met someone to who I was attracted and who shared similar interests and values. You made me laugh and accepted me for me. The more time we spent together, the more I realized I wanted to always have you in my life.

With each obstacle we overcame together and each fight we worked through, I grew closer and closer to you. I could be vulnerable around you because you made me feel safe. We accept each other's imperfections. Therefore, we are perfectly imperfect together.

I listen to some people who describe their love life as boring and repetitive. I am so lucky. We talk about and share our desires. We are there for each other even when one isn't quite in the mood. I guess that's why they call them quickies. But there is love and passion. It helps to know what the other likes and dislikes. I love the safety and security of a monogamous marital bed. I love it when you still flirt with me years into our marriage. I still long for your touch..your caresses, and the passion and fire it can fill me with. I feel so desired and wanted.

My love, I never knew I could love you as much as I do. I now know what love means. I hope it continues to grow year after year.

Your True Love

First Child

Nevermore in love

Then holding your very first child

While holding each other

Perfect Start

A clamoring alarm startled her from a restless sleep. Half asleep, her feet slowly exit the covers. Then, hitting the crisp air, they make a hasty retreat.

She rolls over and hits the snooze on the alarm. She adjusts her pillow and pulls the covers under her chin. Then slowly dozes off again. She shuts the alarm off two more times. On the third time, Her husband, who woke on the first alarm, walks into the room with his hair uncombed, bare-chested, and just his dress pants.

Along with his fresh shower scent is the aroma of coffee. He sets it on her nightstand. Gently he crawls into bed next to her. As he softly caresses her face, he admires the one he loves. He smiles at her as she struggles to get out of bed and in all her natural beauty. His hands run through her hair as he whispers softly into her ears.

Under his gentle persuasion, she slowly opens her eyes. At this moment, the world seems like a lifetime away. Yet, as time seems to stand still, she is overwhelmed by his love. Caressing her face, he whispers of his love and her beauty. Warm and safe in his arms, she wishes this moment would not end. What a perfect start!

The clamoring alarm sounds for the fourth and final time. Reality hits! She is forced to emerge from the covers. Her eyes have bags, and her hair is messier than usual due to her restless night. She grabs the coffee on her way to wake her children.

She makes breakfast, prepares lunches, and sets out their clothes as they wake. She finds the book bags, shoes, and last night's misplaced homework. The children bicker and fight as they try to prepare for school. Finally, she jumps in the shower, does her hair, and gets ready for work. There is no time to think but to do. They must not be late for work or school.

Each morning is the same hurried routine. She curses the rushing and the chaos. Swearing that tomorrow, she'd get up on the first buzz. After the long lights and heavy traffic, she finally gets the kids dropped off at school. The work parking lot is full, and she has to park far. Rain starts pouring. She looks in the back seat and realizes she never put the umbrella back into the car

She takes a moment to reflect when she gets to her desk soaking wet. Why can't her day be like her perfect start?

True Love

Trust

Respect

Understanding

Express

Listen

Open-hearted

Validate

Exonerate

Kiss

A mom kisses her child goodnight.

A little boy sits on his dad's lap to give a hug and kiss.

Grandma kisses her family as they come for a visit.

A kiss on the cheek from an old friend

A sixteen-year-olds first kiss

The anxious kiss of a first date

The first kiss as husband and wife

The first-morning kiss of a fiftieth anniversary

The quick hello and goodbye kiss

Eyes of love meet before the romantic kiss

Slow dancing and kissing

The kiss of fire and passion

The kiss of friends moving away

The last kiss of a breakup

The kiss on the forehead of a sick child.

The last kiss before a loved one leaves this life.

Romantic Night

Years of marriage have brought comfort to each day.
The romance seemed like a part of yesterday.
Our love was unseen.
Our lives became routine.

You surprised me in a new way.
A babysitter you found that day.
We dressed in our finest clothes.
Where we were going, I did not know.

We went to a nice restaurant by the bay.
In a small private room, a waiter took us without delay.
The dimly lit room had a flower, soft music, and candlelight.
This was a dinner like no other night.

There was nothing that was to my dismay.
The dinner was perfect in every way.
I chose items off the menu that were new.
You wanted something different, so you did too.

Soft, loving words you did say.
I was being romanced like no other day.
Reaching across the table, you gently caressed my cheek.
The feelings made my insides grow weak.

Our eyes joined across the candlelit way.
I could see the flickering in your eyes that day.
I wondered if the fire was from the candlelight
Or was it from the fire raging inside you that night?

As dinner ended, I thought it was the end of the day.
But to my surprise, there was more along the way.
You had planned for a nice hotel room.
There the fire of our love was consumed.

In our room that overlooked the bay,
We snuggled as we watched the colorful sunset to end the day.
Sailboats glistened on the water's edge.
On that day, you rekindled the love you pledged.

Priceless

the flaws

are

what makes

the

artwork

hung

in a

home

unique

and

priceless

Parent's Night

Baths, brushing teeth, bedtime story
The little ones finally nestled in a bed
Thoughts of being with you locked in my head
Time slowly ticks while waiting for the children to sleep

Heavy eyes turn to sleep
Being held in your sweet embrace
My heart starts to race
The hectic day melts away

A beautiful night of heat and passion
Love fills the air
The world doesn't exist, not a worry, not a care
Two cuddled into one

Time quickly ticks while we know the children will wake
Thoughts of being with you locked in my head
The little ones will emerge from bed

Breakfast, brushing teeth, begin dressing

Life-Time Friends

Patience and kindness

Patience and Love

As I struggled to work through the past

You stayed by my side, never judging

As I struggled to deal with the pressures of the day

You allowed me to talk and work through it

As I struggled with miscommunication

You were willing to sit down and explain and allow me to explain

As I had issues with some of the things you did

You apologized, and we worked out compromises we could agree

As I failed you and wasn't perfect

You loved me for me

As problems slammed us from all sides

You worked with me to get through or around them

As I needed to laugh

You were silly and goofy, and I didn't have a chance to be serious

As I wanted someone to do things with

You went to be with me despite the activity

As I needed to feel love

You gave a gentle touch or passion as needed

You did these things and more

I gave back to you the same, if not more

We trusted each other

We enjoyed being with each other

We laughed and played together

We were special because we treated each other special

We share love, but what makes us special

Is that we are lifetime friends.

From the Heart

When we first dated, hiding a fart

Was a creative work of art,

Disguising the smell,

Blaming and never tell

Now burps and farts come from the heart.

Twelve Roses

When I walked into the house today,
I saw a gorgeous vase on the table
It had the baby's breath and a card on display
Inside it read, "find the flowers if you are able."

One lay on a table nearby in plain site
There was a card attached to a string
Inside it said. "You are my everything.
Find another by candle lite."

To the fireplace, I did go
Another rose and a note
What a way for his love to show
This one talked of the love he would always devote.

Each clue took me to a new place
I raced to find each one to see
His kind words about why he loved me
Each note brought a tear to my face

One flower at a time filled my vase
This was a fantastic way to show his love
He is a remarkable man who can't be replaced
He is my love that was sent from above.

Spouse

Spouse

Devoted, honest

Loving, doting accepting

Can't live without

Mate

Anniversary

We celebrate our love on our anniversary day.

God had given us a love to stay.

He joined two different views.

In our troubles, one of us has known what to do.

We have had our struggles each day.

Loving you has added sparkle along the way.

It had taken time to adjust to our married life.

It was not easy going from being single to husband and wife.

We had to learn to join our finances and bills.

Along with it came many emotional hills.

There were many good times during our married years.

We talked through those times of tears.

There were many surprises about you I had not known.

But by understanding, we have grown.

I want to show my love in so many ways.

And I look forward to celebrating more anniversary days.

Positive

Not perfect

Never amount to anything

Nothing I do is right

Not good enough

These are words foreign to me

In my heart and mind,

you are everything to me.

You're my heart, my soul, My life.

You do all the right things to make me feel loved

You are more than enough for me.

Together we can accomplish anything

I am with the perfect person for me

Through the Years

Looking back upon our lives
We had heartache
And Pain
Looking back upon our lives
We had Joy
And Laughter
Looking back upon our lives
We face pain together
And faced it apart
Looking back upon our lives
We were best friends
And we had best friends
Looking back upon our lives
We trusted each other
And shared
Looking back upon our lives
We wronged the other
And we apologized
Looking back upon our lives
We loved each other deeply
And we loved ourselves
Looking back upon our lives
We did things together
And we did stuff apart
Looking back upon our lives
We had our responsibilities
And we helped the other
Looking back upon our lives
We were us
And we were ourselves

Time Stands Still

Christmas at Grandma
Entering the house
The first thing that hits you
The smell of pastries baking
Mixed with the smell of pine
From the Christmas Tree
With the twinkling lights
The shimmering of the silver tinsel
Christmas music plays in the background
While all the kids laugh as they pull taffy
Grandpa gathering kids in circles
By age and gender
He throws presents in the middle
Everyone takes one
Kids frantically open present
Some smile with excitement
Others moan as they see someone
With a better present
Some exchange it with another kid
Hot pies sit on the counter
Everyone sitting around the dinner table
Or claims their places on the couches and chairs
All the other kids will sit on the floor
That is set like a buffet which consists
of an assortment of plates, cups,
saucers and silverware
One of the adults will fill the kid's cups
Kool-Aid was the only choice
Adults could have soda, Kool-Aid, or coffee

Meanwhile, Grandma places Turkey on the table
Followed by all the trimmings
All the adults will make the plates for the kids
Once the kids are settled on the floor and
Living Room Furniture
The adults will settle in around the table
There are no assigned seats
Yet they all know their place
Everyone is talking to the relatives
They haven't seen in a while and
The ones they see every day.
Finally, eating the dessert
Homemade pies and cakes
Served with vanilla ice cream.
Time goes by fast and the evening ends
Time stands still in your childhood memories

Until We Meet Again

A love like ours never ends
It's "until I see you again."

Index of Titles

"Love is like a friendship caught on fire. In the beginning a flame, very pretty, often hot and fierce, but still only light and flickering. As love grows older, our hearts mature and our love becomes as coals, deep-burning and unquenchable."

-Bruce Lee

Y

About the Author

Deborah Ann Martin is a poet and blogger of www.survivinglifelessons.com. She is a single mom of four adult children and has four grandchildren. She has been writing poetry for as long as she remembers. Deborah gains her inspiration from the crazy events of her life and the life she observes around her. She earned her MBA during her unique career path. She is a veteran and is currently working as Computer Application Administrator. Her unique work and life have given her the knowledge and inspiration to write. This book is the first in a series.

She enjoys her adventures and family. She recently bought a house and is enjoying the experience of fixing it up to what she wants. At 55, she is in the dating stage of the love cycle. She hopes to one day find her true love.

www.ingramcontent.com/pod-product-compliance
Lightning Source LLC
LaVergne TN
LVHW051247080426
835513LV00016B/1790